*Small bison herd digging through snow to feed in meadow near Topping Point on the north shore of Yellowstone Lake*

Bison most often use their faces to move snow away from buried forage, although they sometimes use their front feet as well. It is common for them to extend their feeding pits outward from their initial excavations, taking advantage of the established edges along the sides of the pits to facilitate further excavations. The scooped out pits they leave behind make for interesting patterns in the snowscapes, and it's also interesting that the feeding areas match up with the best quality forage available for the buffalo – as revealed when the snow melts in the spring.

*Cross country skiers Chris Gastrock and Jill Waters looking at bison while on backcountry ski trip in Hayden Valley*

Hardy beasts that they are, bison manage to winter over in Yellowstone's beautiful but harsh Hayden Valley. To do so, the animals make use of windblown and mostly snow free ridge tops in the valley, and also by frequenting the valley's thermal areas. The buffalo in this photograph are taking advantage of the reduced snow cover along a small geothermal runoff stream. Chris and Jill were fortunate enough to be able to observe this buffalo herd because they made the effort to ski out to where the animals like to spend a good portion of their winter.

*Small herd of pronghorns filing across wintry landscape near Landslide Creek*

Pronghorns as a species are millions of years old, and when European Americans first entered their range they numbered at least 15 million animals. By the early 20th century, however, their population had dwindled to as few as 13,000 individuals. Yellowstone National Park is one of the few places where the species survived from prehistoric times until the present. Because of their small stature and spindly legs, and because they rely on their great speed to evade predators, Yellowstone's pronghorns migrate to the park's lowest elevations in the winter to escape the deep snows that fall in higher portions of the park. Landslide Creek is just inside the park's northern boundary near the gateway community of Gardiner, Montana.

*Antler Peak and other mountains in the Gallatin Range from Swan Lake Flat*

Firnspiegel is a German word that literally translated means "old snow mirror." Such snow forms when the sun melts the surface of a snowpack, and the melted snow subsequently refreezes into a thin layer of ice that creates a reflective surface. Firnspiegel is shining off the mountains in this photograph. An interesting sidebar in the history of the Yellowstone region is that firnspiegel might very well have been the reason the Rocky Mountains were once known as the "Shining Mountains." Captain Meriwether Lewis was looking at the Rockies not far north of the present day park on July 4, 1805 when he wrote in his journal "I have thought it probable that these mountains might have derived their appellation of shining [sic] Mountains, from their glittering appearance when the sun shines in certain directions on the snow which covers them."

*Jeff Henry removing blocks of snow from roof of Canyon General Store*

Because of regional topography and other factors, the Yellowstone Plateau receives colossal amounts of snow. During heavy winters truly awesome amounts of snow accumulate on park buildings, as pictured here. Snowpack weights of well over 200 pounds per square foot of roof surface are frequently calculated – and this on buildings usually designed for much smaller load limits. One consequence is that the park has a long history of buildings collapsing under such enormous weights, or in more common instances suffering damage short of outright collapse. Ever since the winter of 1880-81, winterkeepers have worked to clear snow loads from the roofs of park structures.

*Bull bison near Elk Antler Creek at sunrise*

This large bull bison had just arisen from his bed on the top of a wind-scoured hill between Trout Creek and Elk Antler Creek in Hayden Valley. He was doing what most creatures do upon arising from sleep.

*Sunrise over Fishing Bridge at 30 below zero*

The present incarnation of Fishing Bridge was built in 1937, following an earlier bridge with the same name that was located a short distance upstream on the Yellowstone River. For decades the bridge was a favorite spot for anglers to fish for Yellowstone's cutthroat trout. By the 1970s, however, the area under the bridge had been identified as a spawning ground for the native fish. There were also problems with traffic congestion and overcrowding among the fishermen, so fishing from the bridge and in nearby waters was banned in 1973. I think it safe to say that no one was contemplating fishing from the bridge or anywhere else in its vicinity on the frigid morning this picture was taken.

*Sunrise over Yellowstone Lake near Topping Point*

This was an extremely cold morning on the north shore of Yellowstone Lake. The beauty, the shadows, the colorful sunlight, the mystery of it all – the cold was not the only thing that was breathtaking that morning.

*Park visitors and Fountain Geyser on extremely cold afternoon*

A Fountain eruption comes in a series of bursts, often beginning as a large bubble of blue water that explodes as it rises up and out of the geyser's vent. The bursting bubble jets water in all directions, often creating an eruptive column as wide as it is high, although the bursts sometimes reach as high as 80-100 feet and at those times the geyser's height exceeds its breadth. These winter visitors enjoyed an even more special spectacle. The temperature that day stayed well below zero, so large amounts of billowing steam above Fountain's erupting water made the column larger and all the more impressive.

*Thomas Schmidt from Germany photographing Silex Spring*

Yellowstone has been a mecca for photographers for almost 150 years now, and most would agree that the park in winter is even more spectacular than it is in other seasons. As a rule I think the colder the weather the more beautiful the scene, and this day was no exception. Silex is the Latin word that has evolved to mean silica in modern English. Silex Spring is a beautiful blue with multicolored runoff channels leading away from the spring, and it occasionally erupts as a geyser. As with all other geothermal features in Yellowstone, its beauty is enhanced with the profuse steam and exquisite frost crystals that form in cold winter weather.

*Pine marten tracks with sunset light reflecting off the snow near the Grand Canyon of the Yellowstone River*

Here the colored light of sunset was reflecting off a patch of open snow among the long shadows of lodgepole pines and other objects. I love this time of day almost as much as I love the first moments of sunrise. Sunset time can be almost as quiet as sunrise, when most people have already retreated to the indoors as the darkness and cold of a winter night are coming on.

*Bull bison feeding along strip of windblown beach at Mary Bay*

Mary Bay is located on the northeast shore of Yellowstone Lake. Because of the area's prevailing southwesterly winds it is perfectly situated to receive large amounts of driftwood that blow across the lake. The bits of wood protruding above the snow in this picture are quite likely fire kills from the wildfires that have become ever more frequent in the Yellowstone area in recent years. The same southwesterly winds that move driftwood across the lake had blown most of the snow away from the strip where this bull bison was foraging. The beach at Mary Bay is also geothermally influenced, another factor working in the bull's favor by further reducing the depth of the snow where he was feeding.

*Crystal Cassidy with huge block of snow she has just toppled onto a roof*

This was a winter (2016-17) of near record snow accumulation, and in this photograph Crystal was working on clearing the enormous weight from a building at Canyon. The remaining blocks of snow behind Crystal were around seven to eight feet tall, while the block she had just toppled weighed in the neighborhood of 4,000-5,000 pounds. The fallen block fractured into pieces when it hit the roof, after which Crystal was able to push the smaller and lighter chunks down and off the roof.

*Cross country skier near Cascade Lake*

Cross country skiing as a way to get around when the snow is deep arrived in the Yellowstone area in the late 1800s. In almost all snow conditions skiing is faster and energetically more efficient than snowshoeing, as well as aesthetically beautiful once a skier has attained a certain level of proficiency. As can be readily seen, the skier pictured here is highly proficient on her skis.

*Rippled snowscape in Gibbon Meadows*

One word for a rippled snow surface like that pictured here is *sastrugi*. It is a word that originated with Russian but which interestingly came to English through the German, being altered a little as it passed through each successive language. Literally, sastrugi means "frozen snow wave," and the waves of snow in this photograph looked to be exactly that—like waves on a lake that were instantaneously flash frozen in place.

*Old Faithful Geyser erupting at sunrise on a very cold winter morning*

Without any question, Old Faithful is the most famous geyser in the world. It is remarkable how it has faithfully erupted about 20-23 times per day, spewing out 3700-8400 gallons of hot water each time, every day of the year, every year since it was officially "discovered" and named in 1870. To me, the great geyser is even more remarkable in winter, when its 204 degree water explodes into air that is sometimes as cold as 80 or more degrees below the freezing point.

*Bull elk feeding on sagebrush near Undine Falls along Lava Creek*

Sagebrush can be an important winter forage for elk. Among other reasons, it is available in the winter because it is taller than grasses or forbs and therefore sticks up above the snow where elk can reach it without having to dig. Big sagebrush (*Artemisia tridentata*), the type pictured here, is also quite high in protein. This particular bull appeared to be in fine condition when I photographed him in early January.

*Mammoth Hot Springs terraces at sunrise*

Mammoth Hot Springs was a shadowy element in early day chronicles of the American West, often appearing in the journals of mountain men and other explorers with vague references like a mountain of sulfur, or even as a volcano. It is pictured here at sunrise on a cold winter morning with unfrozen geothermal water in the foreground.

*Runoff channels at Mammoth Hot Springs*

With ghostly dead trees and ethereal steam rising from geothermal runoff channels, the Mammoth area is similar to better known geyser basins farther south in Yellowstone National Park. Similar but different, the area is nonetheless intriguing and beautiful in its own right.

*Bison in heavy snowstorm in lower Fairy Meadows*

This photograph was taken in early winter, during the first heavy snowstorm that would accumulate and remain on the ground until it melted the following spring. Such storms marking the onset of true winter used to come reliably during the first week of November, and in the more distant past they seemed to have arrived in late October. In more recent years there have been winters that did not begin until Thanksgiving, and sometimes even later than that. Deep snows and strong cold on the Yellowstone Plateau, along with its remoteness, were factors that combined to save the wild buffalo from extinction in the United States in the late 19th and early 20th centuries. Indeed, Yellowstone is the only place in the United States where wild buffalo persisted from prehistoric times right up until the present.

*Mattie Culver's gravestone at the site of the Marshall Hotel*

This gravestone is located on the west side of present day Nez Perce Picnic Area about 10 miles north of Old Faithful, and it marks one of the saddest stories in Yellowstone's history. Mattie Culver was the wife of winterkeeper Ellery C. Culver at the Marshall Hotel at the mouth of Nez Perce Creek when she died of tuberculosis on March 2, 1889. Mattie left behind not only her husband but also their 18 month old daughter Theda. After her death Mattie's husband had to place her in two barrels connected end to end to keep scavengers away from her body until he could gouge a grave into the frozen ground near the hotel. Because Mattie died in the winter I have always thought that pictures of her oft-photographed grave are most fittingly shot during that season of the year. It was exceptionally cold the morning I shot this photograph, and the light was somber.

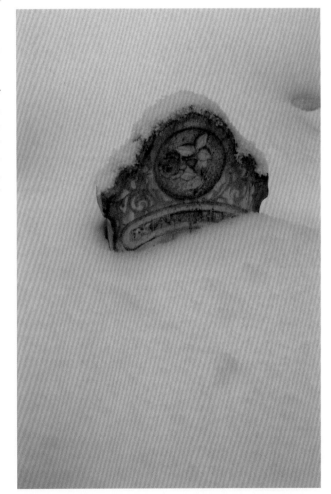

*Tour guide leading a group of snowshoers through the Upper Geyser Basin*

Tour guides were an integral element on the Yellowstone scene even before the area was designated a national park. In a sense the mountain men and other frontiersmen who guided the first official explorers into what is now the park in the early 1870s were tour guides, as were Indians who guided the mountain men themselves when the latter first showed up on the scene. Many of today's tour guides carry a lifelong commitment to the area, and work their jobs with rare levels of passion and devotion. Karl Swaboda was the guide leading his group on a snowshoe tour of the Upper Geyser Basin on this cold and steamy winter morning.

*Fire-killed spruce tree along the Mallard Lake trail near Old Faithful*

This tree was killed by the great North Fork Fire on September 7, 1988, the same day the fire famously swept through the Old Faithful area. Although the scorched bark on the tree had long since peeled off, charring can be seen around the knots that were recessed into the trunk. Furrows bored into the wood by insects were also present, while regenerating forest was in the background on either side of the dead tree trunk.

*Cross country skiers on a trek through Hayden Valley on a stormy winter day*

Ominously dark storm clouds can be seen in the distance beyond this line of skiers who were traveling single file in the trail broken by the leader of the procession. Many species of wildlife resort to the same energy saving technique when traveling through deep snow. Snow layers were weakly bonded on the day this photograph was shot – all around us we could hear and sometimes see the snowpack collapse because of the disturbance our passing created. The curious thing was that in some places there were successive collapses of the snowpack, where the leader of our group would cause an initial settling, but then another skier down the line in our group of six would cause another collapse when he or she passed the same point. Snow conditions were so unstable that day that it would have been foolhardy, perhaps downright suicidal, if we had ventured onto avalanche-prone slopes.

*Snow sculptures on fallen log near Fern Cascades*

These wafer-thin creations were formed when the sun began to melt snow that had accumulated on a fallen log. Snow is an endlessly fascinating substance, both during its accumulation and its melting. Basic inputs from seemingly simple elements like temperature, moisture, and wind combine to create a limitless array of expressions in the snow, such as the line of figures pictured here. To me, they look like a line of parading circus animals in miniature.

**25**

*Jeff Henry and Kris Mangold clearing snow from the roof of a park building*

This photograph was taken by a camera with a timer mounted on a tripod, and it shows us working on a tremendously heavy snowpack that was threatening to damage the building on which it had accumulated. This was an exceptionally heavy winter (1995-96), and by the time this picture was made late in the season the snow had consolidated to the point where it was almost impossible to cut with the crosscut saw that Kris was trying to use. That's why I was using a shovel to chop from above, hoping the added force of the downward motion would give me the advantage I needed to chip away chunks for later removal from the roof.

*Lewis Canyon on a very cold February sunrise*

The naming of the Lewis River has an interesting history. It is named, of course, for Captain Meriwether Lewis of the Lewis and Clark Expedition of 1804-1806. Originally, Lewis and Clark named the entire fork of the Columbia River, the fork we call the Snake River, for Lewis himself. By 1872 Lewis' name had been replaced by the modern name by which we know the river that originates in Yellowstone National Park and flows westward across southern Idaho. In that year a member of one of Yellowstone's first official surveys named Lewis Lake in recognition of Meriwether Lewis as a means of commemorating the great explorer. The name Lewis was later extended to identify the river which feeds into and also drains out of Lewis Lake and then flows as a tributary into the Snake River near Yellowstone's South Entrance. Captain Lewis himself never came closer than about 60 straight line miles from the present park, and so never saw the lake and river that today bear his name. The morning of this photograph was quite cold, and the rising sun had colored the small cloud above the canyon a pastel pink.

*Wind sculpted snow and sunrise colors at Sulphur Spring Creek in Hayden Valley*

This was a fairly cold morning, in the range of 30 below zero, when the sun came up and cast beautiful light and shadows across the snow in Hayden Valley. The snow cornice in the top center of the photograph had been formed by the valley's prevailing southwesterly winds, which often seem incessant. Sulphur Spring Creek itself was buried under several feet of snow in the bottom of the swale that curls along the left side of this picture.

*Cave Falls on the Fall River in early winter*

Cave Falls is situated on the Fall River in the Bechler area of Yellowstone, which in turn is located in the southwestern corner of the park. The Bechler area is the most lightly visited portion of Yellowstone, and that is even more true in the winter than in other seasons of the year. The name Fall River is a derivative from the earlier name Falling Fork, which in turn originated with the fabled mountain men of the early 19th century. I took this picture in early winter, when the first of Bechler's legendarily deep snows were beginning to pile up.

*Sunrise over the frozen Lamar River*

This photograph was taken near the Lamar River's confluence with Soda Butte Creek, and just below the slope known as Jackson Grade. The sparse trees on the right side of the frame that partially block the glare of the rising sun are some of the few lodgepole pines that grow on the floor of open Lamar Valley, although most in this particular grove have died in recent years. It was a cold and beautiful morning in what fur trapper Osborne Russell fondly named the "Secluded Valley" in a journal entry in 1836.

*Elk in geothermal steam near Old Faithful Geyser*

Wintering elk were common in the drainages of the Firehole, Gibbon and Madison rivers until about the mid 2000s, when they were reduced to a few surviving individuals along the Madison River near Seven Mile Bridge. The reason for their demise was the reintroduction of wolves to Yellowstone National Park, which began in 1995. Elk wintering in the geyser basins along the above named rivers were contained by deep snow surrounding the geothermal areas, and were unable to escape from the predatory wolves who arrived in the thermal basins shortly after they were released. It is likely that the wintering elk in the Firehole/Gibbon/Madison area were themselves artifacts of human influence in Yellowstone's ecosystem, specifically through the elimination of native wolves in the early part of the 20th century – before then it is unlikely that many elk wintered over in the park's snowbound interior. In that sense the presence of wintering elk in places like the Upper Geyser Basin may have been unnatural, but the stately animals did make for dramatic elements in winter photographs.

*Snow-draped sign at Fishing Bridge*

The Fishing Bridge area bustles with activity in the summer, but all was quiet when I shot this photograph in midwinter. The picture is a good illustration of the tensile strength of snow.

*American coots and trumpeter swans on open water in Mary Bay, Yellowstone Lake*

Because of geothermal outlets there is always open water in Mary Bay, no matter how cold the weather. Waterfowl take advantage of the open water, as pictured here, as do otters who are able to access fish through the open water in the otherwise icebound Yellowstone Lake. Flat Mountain on the left and Mount Sheridan on the right rise above the forests on the other side of the ice covered lake.

*Lake Yellowstone Hotel in a heavy snowstorm*

Lake Hotel is the oldest lodging facility still operating in Yellowstone National Park. It first opened for business in 1891, and since then has undergone many additions, renovations and other alterations. At times, bureaucratic machinations even threatened to demolish and remove it altogether. Fortunately for us, the lovely hotel still exists in its equally lovely setting on the north shore of Yellowstone Lake. All my life I have been mesmerized by snow falling in windless conditions – there is so much motion with the falling flakes that the effect can be dizzying, but in spite of all the movement the silence is absolute. Uncountable millions of flakes were swirling down in total silence when I shot this photograph on the lake side of the historic structure.

*The Lower Falls of the Yellowstone River*

At one time the Lower Falls and the Upper Falls a short distance upstream were known collectively as the Great Falls of the Yellowstone River. Early references to the falls go back at least as far as 1806, when based on Indian information Captain Meriwether Lewis made mention of them in his journal. In winter, spray from the Lower Falls freezes into the massive accumulation that can be seen just to the left of the falling cascade. The sound of the falls in winter mysteriously fades in and out—sometimes inexplicably muted to a low level, at other times ascending to an overwhelming roar.

*Coyote crossing the snowscape in Hayden Valley at sunset*

This photograph was taken on the wide flat between Alum Creek and Sulphur Spring Creek in Hayden Valley. The sun was low and the clouds were colorful, and the colors and shadows were reflected off the vast snowscape.

*Bison and steam with setting sun at Fountain Paint Pot*

Bison often crowd close to geothermal vents in winter for the warmth they provide. Sometimes in jostling for the warmer spots smaller members of the herd are bumped into open hot springs or mudpots—often with scaldingly fatal results. These three buffalo, two of which are visible only as shadows in the mist, bring to mind thoughts of how Native Americans revered both the shaggy animals and the sun, which is also visible as a small orb through the steam near the left side of the photograph.

*Grizzly bear tracks in snow by snowmobile near Potts Hot Spring Basin*

Irrefutably, Yellowstone's grizzly bears stay active much longer into the fall than they used to do. Nowadays many bears stay out and about well into what is clearly the winter season, as can be seen by these tracks near my snowmobile. I was on my way from Old Faithful to Bridge Bay Marina to do some roof clearing work in December when I came across these tracks, as I and many others have come across similar tracks at the same advanced season of the year in recent times. Reasons why the bears stay out longer are probably several, but one of the biggest factors has to be Yellowstone's increasingly milder climate, in which the onset of winter is substantially later than it used to be.

*Grizzly bear tracks in front of the Old Faithful Inn*

As grizzly bears stay active later into the autumn and early winter than they used to, so also do they arise from hibernation earlier in the spring. I worked on a carcass survey for a grizzly bear study project for many springs in the 1980s and 1990s, in which I walked the thermal basins along the Firehole River valley in search of winterkilled elk and bison and then kept track of which carcasses grizzly bears utilized for food. In those days I consistently found the first bear tracks of the year within one day of March 25, which not surprisingly coincided with the peak period of die off for wintering ungulates. In recent years some bears have emerged as early as the first week of February, undoubtedly another sign of a warming Yellowstone.

*Keena Lewis and Mariah Gale Henry winterkeeping the Canyon General Store*

These two girls, both 11 years old at the time of the photograph, were checking the size of the pile of snow they have accumulated under the eaves of the building. Most observers think that winterkeeping requires a lot strength. Strength is an asset, for sure, but technique and finesse are far more important, as evidenced by the size of the pile of snow blocks on the ground that Keena and Mariah had amassed before this photo was snapped – the pile by then was less than three feet below the eaves of the roof.

*Cross country ski instructor Jenny Wolfe with pupil Maddie Jonkel during ski lesson at Old Faithful*

Cross country ski lessons are offered at both Old Faithful Snow Lodge and at the Mammoth Hot Springs Hotel. In all probability, this was Maddie Jonkel's first lesson, and she was fortunate to have a skier as accomplished as Jenny Wolfe as an instructor. This photo was shot at Old Faithful, near the Snow Lodge.

*Lines of Canada geese tracks in Pocket Basin along the Firehole River*

Pocket Basin is well named – it is a concavity in the low hills around it with its rim forming a horseshoe that opens toward the Firehole River. Its shape makes sense when you understand that the concavity was created by a steam explosion, when underground water heated to the point where it flashed to steam and exploded outward at an oblique angle. Pocket Basin is located a short distance up the Firehole from the better known Ojo Caliente Spring, and is situated on the same side of the river. There are many interesting geothermal features in and near Pocket Basin, with the basin and the area surrounding it serving as winter range for a number of animals both large and small. These geese left their tracks in a skiff of snow that had fallen the night before and which was sure to melt because of the warmth of the geothermal ground, along with added warmth from the rising sun. The geese had been in the basin before I arrived, perhaps to consume some of the crushed geyserite as grit for their crops, or perhaps to dabble in some of the area's many geothermal runoff channels.

*Sunrise shining through dead snags and regrowth from 1988's Wolf Lake Fire*

The dead trees in this photograph were killed in late August of 1988 by the Wolf Lake Fire, which itself was an offshoot of the much larger North Fork Fire. Actually, the Wolf Lake Fire was merely a bureaucratic designation intended to make management of the two massive fires a bit easier. The forest was regenerating nicely when this photograph was taken, and the sunrise light was beautifully colored. The strips of open snowscapes that can be seen in the distance are parts of Yellowstone's famous Hayden Valley, while the line of mountains in the farther distance are the Absarokas, which in that sector approximate the eastern boundary of the Yellowstone National Park as well as the eastern boundary of the immense Yellowstone caldera.

*Old Faithful Inn in geothermal mist at sunrise*

The Old House of the Inn, the portion pictured here, first opened for business in June of 1904, and so is well over 100 years old. It is remarkable the great building has been able to weather extremes such as the cold of this misty morning. And it's not just the cold – the building also has been able to withstand crushing snow loads, along with hot, dry summers and the damaging rays of the sun at this high elevation. Old Faithful Inn also survived the Hebgen Lake Earthquake on August 17, 1959 and the North Fork Fire on September 7, 1988, the latter being a very close call indeed. Beyond all that, there were times in Yellowstone's history when park managers considered tearing down the Inn and replacing it with visitor facilities elsewhere. Fortunately wiser points of view prevailed, and it is also a testament to those who were assigned to maintain the Inn that it still exists today.

*Patterns on the snowscape in Hayden Valley in the Crater Hills*

In a very real sense the patterns on this snowscape are tracings of the wind. It's obvious that the prevailing wind blows up the back of the ridge in the foreground, around the end of the ridge to the left, and then horizontally across the frame before exiting to the right. It's fascinating to me to ponder such tangible evidence left behind by the otherwise invisible element.

*Old Faithful Geyser and lodgepole pines at sunrise on a 40 below zero morning*

As always, the colder it is in Yellowstone the more beautiful the conditions. For me, this was close to perfect – extreme cold, clear skies, with Old Faithful in eruption right at sunrise. The Old Faithful Inn is also visible in the distance, between some of the lodgepole saplings in the lower right third of the photograph.

*Bison passing by erupting
Sawmill Geyser at sunset*

Sawmill Geyser is located near the boardwalk across the Firehole River from the better-known Castle Geyser, and only a half mile or so down the river from Old Faithful. Sawmill is well situated for nicely backlit photographs at sunset. This bison was one of several grazing on the snowfree ground in the area. As I watched, members of the herd passed single file along the concentric rims of geyserite surrounding the geyser as they moved upriver. I was lucky enough to be in the right place at the right time to silhouette this animal against the setting sun.

*Silhouettes of ghost trees in Biscuit Basin*

Ghost trees form in cold weather, most often in early to mid-winter when the sun is so low in the sky that it lacks the power to melt accumulated frost from the trees during the daytime. Usually the ghostly deposits form when wafting geothermal steam accretes on the limbs and foliage of nearby trees over a period of several days. Sometimes falling snow also accumulates onto limbs and needles, and adds its bulk to the frost that has already coalesced into place. In extended periods of cold weather, as happened more frequently in the past, the accumulations grow to the point where they can break limbs. Many Yellowstone observers, including this one, really do imagine the forms of spectral beings in the frosty shapes of ghost trees.

*Winterkeeper Jim McBride removing large blocks of snow from the roof of Lake Yellowstone Hotel*

Strong winter winds blow prodigious amounts of snow across Yellowstone Lake and onto the Lake Yellowstone Hotel. The snow Jim McBride is moving here had drifted on some flat roofs on the lee side of the building, where it had accumulated in a deep and thoroughly consolidated mass. Jim was a winterkeeper in the Lake Area, at various times at the Lake Lodge and the Lake Hotel, from 1986 until his retirement in 2007.

*Snowshoer on trek in Hayden Valley*

I have always been intrigued by the contrast between snowshoes and cross-country skis, two very different responses to the fundamental problem of moving around when the snow is deep. In most snow conditions skis are much preferable to snowshoes, at least in my opinion, although snowshoes do have their uses. This is especially true in the realm of roof shoveling work in Yellowstone, where snowshoes are useful for moving ladders and tools from building to building. I also have to admit a partiality for snowshoes because of their association with indigenous North Americans. This picture is a good illustration of the winter harshness of Hayden Valley with its vast windswept snowscapes. The snow near the snowshoer's feet in this photograph had been particularly textured by the wind, and overall the photograph suggests the cold wildness of the place where it was shot.

*Snowshoe hare hiding at base of lodgepole pine seedling*

Although rarely seen, snowshoe hares are a common species in Yellowstone. They have a special affinity for young forests, such as those that have been regenerating since the great fires of 1988. It's much more common to see snowshoe tracks than it is to see the animals themselves, but on this day I was lucky enough to spot this one crouched among some lodgepole pine seedlings that had sprouted in the wake of 1988's Wolf Lake Fire, near Virginia Cascades on the Gibbon River.

*Large bull bison silhouetted by the setting sun, near Frog Rock*

Frog Rock is a glacial boulder on northern Yellowstone's Blacktail Plateau. It can look like a crouching frog complete with a frog face, especially in certain light conditions and most especially with certain patterns of snow deposition on the rock. This was a beautiful December sunset with just the right degree of cloudiness. The hill barely visible in the distance behind the bull is Bunsen Peak near Mammoth Hot Springs.

*Dead lodgepole pine and windblown snowscape*

This tree near the east end of the Mary Mountain trail in Hayden Valley was killed by the Wolf Lake Fire in late August of 1988. When I photographed it at sunrise years later the wind had left beautiful etchings in the snowscapes around it. Coincidentally, I also have photographs of the area around this tree while it was burning in 1988 – I have been very, very fortunate to have spent as much time in Yellowstone as I have, to have had the opportunity to see the progressions of such natural phenomena as great wildfires and the succession of many winters.

*Wolf tracks in geyserite along the Firehole River in the Lower Geyser Basin*

These tracks were the result of another fascinating progression of natural phenomena. First a wolf came by in warmer weather, when the finely crushed geyserite underfoot was wet and soft. The wolf left tracks imprinted in the soft substrate, which later froze when the temperature chilled. Then came a light fall of snow, which was followed by a wind of just the right intensity so that the surrounding light snow blew away but snow recessed into the tracks remained. The result was this beautifully highlighted line of tracks.

*Wolf tracks in geyserite and photographer's hand in the Norris Geyser Basin*

No matter how many times I come across wolf tracks I am always struck by their enormous size. I think most people have the same deep-seated response, a response not just rooted in the awesome size of the tracks, but also related to the other powerful feelings associated with the evocative animals that made them.

*Ryan Hirzig and Mike Cordes winterkeeping the Old Faithful Inn from a man lift*

In several respects, winterkeeping in Yellowstone's past was simpler than it is today. Back in the day caretakers had only to be concerned with removing enough snow so that the buildings in their charge didn't collapse under the great weight. Nowadays there are many park buildings that are heated in winter, and massive ice dams along the eaves of such buildings are one result. The Inn is not open in winter, but this particular year it was heated for the sake of an interior renovation project. Ryan and Mike were charged with preventing leakage to the inside of the building by smashing the icicles and ice dams along the eaves to facilitate drainage of further meltwater flowing down the roof from above. To do the work safely they employed the use of a man lift.

*Wolf-killed bison carcass on the snowscape near Elk Antler Creek in Hayden Valley*

All the tracks and blood spots in the foreground show where a wolf pack was nearing the end of their chase to bring down one of Yellowstone's bison. The small dark spot on the snow in the background is the carcass. The natural world is a tapestry, with elements like birth and death, beauty and threat, peace and pain all intertwined.

*Penta Geyser erupting at winter sunset in the Upper Geyser Basin*

Historically, Penta Geyser has been irregular, sometimes playing with intervals as short as two and a half hours, at other times going entire summers with only two or three observed eruptions. The geyser's vent is only a few feet from the boardwalk, so for a observer fortunate enough to be on hand for a Penta eruption the experience can be much more intimate than it is with most other geysers. I was lucky to catch the geyser erupting right at the key moment of sunset when I shot this photograph.

*Lamar Valley creased with large numbers of elk tracks on a winter sunrise*

Elk used to winter in large numbers in Yellowstone's Lamar Valley, but nowadays most of the animals move farther north to lower elevations along the Yellowstone River valley. Large herds still pass through Lamar, however, en route to the winter range they now prefer. That's what had happened here – apparently big herds of the big animals had crossed the valley the night before I shot this photograph. I didn't see the animals themselves, but it was still a thrill to see all the signs they had left behind in their passing.

*Patterns on ice and snow, shortly after
Yellowstone Lake freezeup*

Yellowstone Lake usually freezes in late December or early January, and then thaws in May or June of the following spring. This photograph was taken from Topping Point, which is the point of land that juts into the lake in front of Lake Lodge. There is often a preliminary freezing or two before the final seize up, with southwesterly winds breaking up the first ice cover and piling up the broken chunks along the north and east shores of the lake. Ridges formed from such broken ice can be seen in this picture, as can the pristine surface of new ice that will probably last until spring. Imposing Mount Sheridan, named for Civil War general Philip Sheridan, can be seen in the distance.

*Mist flowing off the plateau and into the Grand Canyon of the Yellowstone River*

Etymologically the word "mist" is related to "mysterious," and in my mind that's exactly what mist is. Mist responds to subtle changes in temperature, ambient humidity, wind, and other factors, and as a result wafts about unpredictably. Here some slight difference between the air in the canyon and the air on the neighboring plateau had caused the mist that formed over the upland during the night to flow downward into the canyon. Such natural processes are mysterious indeed, and always fascinating.

*Snowmobiles on the West Entrance Road*

Management changes in recent years have restricted snowmobile access to Yellowstone to the point where most riders have to come into the park as part of a guided tour. This tour had just entered the park from West Yellowstone, Montana when I snapped the photograph near Mount Jackson.

*The Absaroka Mountain chain east of Yellowstone Lake, in twilight after winter sunset*

The Absaroka Mountains are an important subchain of the Rockies. Named for the Indians we now call the Crows, they approximate the east boundary of Yellowstone National Park for a substantial part of their length, and they were the setting for many important events in the history of the American West. The mountains were photographed in this frame from the north shore of Yellowstone Lake, with the ice covered lake in the foreground and a cloud bank colored with pastel reflections of the postsunset glow in the western sky.

*Sunrise shining through lodgepole pine forest near LeHardy's Rapids*

To me, these beautiful shadows and light serve to illustrate the nature of Yellowstone's signature tree species – how they tend to grow so straight and tall, in thick stands, and in a wintry environment. One of the many reasons I like photographing in winter is the way shadows are so apparent on the clean snowscapes.

*A wickiup in a secluded glen on Yellowstone's Northern Range*

Wickiups were conical structures built by standing up a number of small poles with their tops leaning against each other. They were constructed by pre-reservation era Indians, and therefore were probably built before 1880 or so. Because of Yellowstone's cold, dry climate, a number of these structures remained standing until very recent times, although most if not all known wickiups have now collapsed. One theory as to their use was that they were built by small parties of Indians out on raiding forays into enemy territory, and the purpose of the structure was to seal in firelight so as not to give away the presence of raiding interlopers. This line of thinking fits with the location where many of the structures were located – in out of the way places where a glint of firelight escaping through cracks in the wickiup would not be seen, and the telltale whiff of drifting woodsmoke likewise not detected.

*Wolf tracks in early season snow along the icy Yellowstone River near Nez Perce Ford*

Nez Perce Ford was named because that's where the Indians of that tribe forded the Yellowstone River during their 1877 flight from the United States Army. For many years prior to the present designation of the ford, which is the most fordable place on the Yellowstone for many miles in either direction, these riffles in the river were known as Buffalo Ford. A party of park rangers on ski patrol came up with the latter name when they spotted a herd of drowned bison at the ford. The dead animals probably had broken through the ice in some deeper part of the river upstream, and after the ice broke up in warming weather the carcasses drifted downstream until they lodged in the shallower water of the ford. The morning this photograph was taken was cold, and ice was beginning to run in the river in advance of the time when the river would seize up completely.

*Winterkeeping work in progress at Canyon*

I skidded this one block of snow out from the snowpack, and then photographed it standing by itself in an attempt to convey a sense of scale for both the mass of the snow on the roof and the scope of the work involved in cutting it into manageable blocks and then skidding the blocks off the roof. Clearing such a roof in years of heavy snow, such as the year pictured here, is a considerable task.

*Dried stalk of an umbrella flower left over from the previous summer, casting shadow on snow*

These lovely little flowers are creamy white in summer. This scene was also lovely in its simplicity – a dried flower stalk protruding above the snow and casting a long shadow across the clean whiteness in the low angle winter light.

*Cross country skiers Ken Keenan and Melissa Stringham skiing past Celestine Pool*

This was a beautiful combination of elements coming together with just the right timing. Ken and Melissa are superb skiers, while the sunset light shining through the steam above Celestine Pool was about as good as it gets. Just a few minutes earlier the light would have been too high in the sky and too far to the viewer's left to make the picture, and a few minutes later the sun would have been down below the southwestern horizon for the night.

*Bison along Yellowstone Lake at Concretion Cove*

Concretion Cove is located on the west end of Mary Bay and a short distance from Indian Pond. It received its name from the unusually shaped concretions that originally were found there in great numbers, but which disappeared through the years because of collection by souvenir hunters. The lodgepole pine in this picture was casting variegated shadows on the snow in the foreground of the photograph, and illustrates that the species can indeed grow in a bushy form if it grows in the open where there is room for its limbs to spread.

*Wildlife biologists Chris Kenyon and Claire Gower with wolf-killed elk carcass in Biscuit Basin*

Chris and Claire often referred to themselves as "the luckiest girls in the world" because of the job they had tracking wolves, elk and bison in the Madison/Firehole/Gibbon river complex. A large part of their dream job was detective work, trying to figure out the hows and whys of what happened between predator and prey.

*Wildlife biologist Matt Becker using telemetry equipment to track radio collared elk near the Porcupine Hills*

Matt was a coworker of the two women pictured in the previous photograph. He never told me, but I strongly suspect that he considered himself as lucky to be employed where he was and doing what he was doing as the two "luckiest girls in the world." It was a very cold morning when I took this photograph, and probably no one else was within miles of me and Matt when I shot it.

*Red fox tracks on the ice of Hazle Lake*

Hazle Lake is a small thermally influenced lake on the north side of the Norris Geyser Basin and just south of Frying Pan Spring. It is geothermally influenced but not to the extent that it doesn't freeze, as can be seen here. The fox tracks made an interesting string across the frosty ice.

*Old Faithful Geyser erupting on a 35 below zero sunrise*

This was an unusually cold morning in that it occurred in March during a winter that overall was quite mild. The first rays of the rising sun colored the erupting column beautifully. It was one of those fortunate times when the famous geyser went off right at sunrise, the air was clear, and I happened to be in the right place at the right time.

*Cross country skier Jenny Wolfe in Biscuit Basin at sunset*

This was an evening that was beautiful beyond words – a skier so skilled that she is downright artful on her skis, ghost trees that had formed around geothermal outlets from an extended period of cold weather, and a gorgeous sunset. It was one of those times when I wished I could freeze the moment, but of course it passed on as surely as the setting sun slid down behind the horizon and cold darkness fell on the geyser basins.

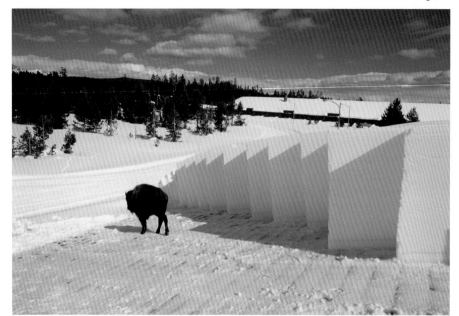

*Young cow bison on the roof of the Canyon General Store*

The winter I shot this photograph (2007-08) was on the heavy side for snowfall, although a long way from being a record. I had cleared about a third of the front of the Canyon General Store when this young cow bison came along and followed my footpath up the snow I had piled up as high as the eaves of the roof. She then spent 45 minutes or so on the roof before descending on the trail she had used to come up. I had seen many wolf tracks in the area over the previous few days, and my interpretation of the buffalo's behavior was that quite likely wolves had broken up a bison herd and left the young female on her own, something that is not likely to happen without some unusual reason. The cow was not fully grown, but she was still a large animal. Her presence on the top of the building gives some perspective on how massive the snow loading on the roof was at the time.

*Bull bison crossing a channel of Tangled Creek in the Lower Geyser Basin*

Tangled Creek derives its name from its many braided stream channels. It has its origin in two very hot lakes, appropriately named Firehole Lake and Hot Lake, but its water cools quite quickly as it flows away from its sources. I have never seen it freeze anywhere along its course, however, and the water most times is warm enough to expose a ribbon of snowfree vegetation along its banks. The snowfree nature of the streamside is attractive to grazing ungulates, such as this big bull bison who was crossing the twisted channels of the creek one cold and foggy morning in midwinter.

*Windblown snowscapes and rising sun near Sulphur Mountain in Hayden Valley*

This hilltop appeared to be especially windblasted when the rising sun caught my eye. I was out on snowshoes looking for just this sort of photograph when everything came together.

*Ice and deep snowbanks along Pelican Creek*

This was an interesting pattern on the snowscapes. The way I read it, the expanse of ice in the foreground must have been open water until not long before I shot the photograph. Perhaps it was kept open by some sort of geothermal activity, but no matter the cause it must have been open water because no snow had accumulated on top of the ice. Then for some reason the geothermal input shut off and the surface of this side channel of Pelican Creek froze, probably in pretty short order. During the time when the water was unfrozen, deep snowbanks piled up on the ground around its margins while the snow that fell on the liquid water simply melted.

*Large herd of buffalo migrating along the Grand Loop Road between Nez Perce Ford and Mud Volcano*

This large herd of bison, only a small portion of which is visible here, migrated out of Pelican Valley and then along park roads to Hayden Valley, from where they continued over Mary Mountain to the valley of the Firehole River. Generally, Yellowstone's bison have been migrating farther and farther north to spend their winters in recent years. In Yellowstone, north in direction generally means down in elevation, but the problem for the bison is that many of them continue to migrate north past the boundary of Yellowstone National Park and into the state of Montana. Once past the boundary they lose the protection of the federal reserve and many are shot by hunters, or captured and shipped to slaughter by the state.

*Bison moving past snowmobilers on the Grand Loop Road near the Mount Holmes trailhead*

These snowmobilers had a head-on encounter with a herd of bison on this section of the Grand Loop Road paralleling Obsidian Creek. Such encounters make winter travel in Yellowstone, whether by snowmobile or other means of winter conveyance, an exciting and unique experience.

*Sawmill Geyser in eruption, with rising sun behind the eruptive column*

Yellowstone, with its splashing geyser water and profuse amounts of geothermal steam, lends itself well to backlit photographs. This picture was shot on a cold and steamy sunrise in midwinter.

*The frozen Yellowstone River at sunrise in Hayden Valley*

All was silent when I shot this photograph of the storied Yellowstone below Grizzly Overlook. The river was completely frozen over, and the vertical riverbank along the left side of the stream was nicely catching the first rays of the rising sun.

*Heavily rimed cottonwood trees along Rose Creek, at the historic Lamar Buffalo Ranch*

This was an extremely cold and frosty morning in Lamar Valley. The building pictured next to the frosty cottonwoods was the bunkhouse for the Lamar Buffalo Ranch, where many of Yellowstone's bison were held captive and to a great degree managed as livestock in the early part of the 20th century in a successful attempt to save the species from extirpation from the park. The bunkhouse is no longer used as sleeping quarters, but instead is shared as a classroom by the Yellowstone Institute and the National Park Service's Expedition Yellowstone, an interpretive program designed for young schoolchildren.

*Lodgepole pine seedlings and sunrise over frozen Yellowstone Lake*

Shortly after freezeup the ice on Yellowstone Lake groans and cracks and makes other curious noises, including a variety of twanging sounds. Locally, the sounds are often referred to as the music of the lake, or the singing of the lake. Personally, some of the sounds the lake makes as the ice heaves and strains remind me of whale songs. The lake was singing the morning I shot this photograph. The morning was perfect – no technology, no machine noise, no other clatter or clutter of the artificial world. During intervals when the ice was quiet there was nothing but the clear vista and the awe-inspiring silence of Yellowstone in midwinter.

*Winterkeepers Dale Fowler and Jim McBride removing snow from the Lake Yellowstone Hotel*

In this photograph, Dale Fowler is on the high part of the hotel, while Jim McBride was picking up the snow Dale was chopping from above and then skidding it off the roof. The winter this picture was taken was not particularly heavy, but the pile of snow on the ground where Jim had been dumping it was nonetheless almost up to the eaves of the roof, which is the roof above the Lake Hotel gift shop and about 12-14 feet high when the ground is bare.

*Jewel Geyser and wintering bison in Biscuit Basin*

These bison were taking advantage of snowfree geothermal ground in Biscuit Basin. A conundrum for wintering ungulates is that the same geothermal influence that leaves the thermal basins snowfree is also largely inhospitable to plant growth, so there is not that much in the way of forage for the animals to eat. The thermal basins are still advantageous, however, and much preferable to plowing through the deep snow found beyond the borders of the basins.

**87**

*Bison feeding on ridgetop in Hayden Valley*

This photograph is a good illustration of how bison use windblown ridges as winter habitat, especially in open areas like Hayden Valley. The prevailing southwesterly wind had blown nearly all the snow off the ridgecrest where the bison are feeding – snowfree grass is actually visible in the picture. The deep drifts in the foreground show where those powerful winds deposited the snow they blew off the windward side as well as the top of the ridge.

*Side channel of Soda Butte Creek near Lamar River trailhead*

Geothermal inflow, such as that from Soda Butte a short distance upstream, had kept some of the water in Soda Butte Creek and its side channels free from ice. Some of the few cottonwood trees that line both the creek and the Lamar River are visible here and there in the frame. The open water had no doubt contributed to the fog that developed over the course of the cold night, as well as to the frost that had been deposited on all exposed surfaces.

*Red fox and snowy bluffs along Elk Antler Creek in Hayden Valley*

I am always amazed at how a small animal like this red fox can survive in the austere immensity of winter in Hayden Valley.

*Red fox tracks and burrowing hole in the snow, on ridge between Trout Creek and Sulphur Mountain*

Fox feet are large in comparison to their body size, and because of this and the fact that they don't weigh much they usually are able to move around on top of the snow. They also dive headfirst through the snow to access rodents living in the subnivean space under the snow and next to the ground. All this is shown here – fox tracks leading up to a spot where the animal torpedoed through the snow and probably killed a mouse or a vole. I have always been fascinated by animal signs, especially animal signs in the snow, and I think figuring out what happened from the signs that have been left behind gives me as much a thrill as sighting the animal itself.

*Trumpeter swans sleeping on ice near the Yellowstone Lake outlet*

This monochromatically white shot was taken on the Yellowstone River near Fishing Bridge. The swans had situated themselves on the ice in a place where it would have been impossible for any predator to approach them without being seen – notice that one swan was awake and had its head up on watch. And the photograph is not completely monochromatic – the darker swan in the lower right corner of the picture was a cygnet of the previous summer.

*Elk crossing the Madison River near Seven Mile Bridge*

All of the elk that used to winter in the Madison, Firehole and Gibbon river valleys have disappeared in recent years except for a small handful that hold on in the vicinity of Seven Mile Bridge, on the Madison River about halfway between Madison Junction and the town of West Yellowstone, Montana. Elk often use water to escape from predatory wolves, wading out to the point where they can stand but the wolves are compelled to swim. The Madison around Seven Mile Bridge is one of the few places in the area where the volume of the stream is sufficient to provide such a refuge.

*Coyote tracks and frost around steaming thermal features in the Mud Volcano area*

The Mud Volcano area is one of the most acidic and also one of the most volatile thermal areas in Yellowstone. Once when making thermal observations while working for the National Park Service I took a break and sat down to rest on some barren thermal ground near the feature in this photograph. At the time I was wearing a pair of brand new pants made of a heavy canvas fabric, but when I looked later in the day I discovered that the acidic earth had eaten holes completely through the seat of the pants, rendering them unusable.

*Winterkeeper Bradley Campbell tossing snow powder into the air*

Winterkeeping, or removing snow from the roofs of buildings in Yellowstone, is exhilarating work. Here my friend Bradley was simply tossing powder snow into the air out of exuberance for the work, and also out of exuberance for the place where he was doing it.

*Elk antlers in the snow along Sedge Creek west of Steamboat Point*

When I first came across these antlers I thought they were sheds, cast off in the spring of the year from the bull who grew them during the previous summer. But on closer examination I could see that the antlers were attached to the skull of the animal, meaning he had died while still wearing the antlers. Further investigation led me to believe that the animal had been killed by wolves. As the area is not winter range for elk, I concluded that most likely the bull had been taken down sometime during the previous autumn, after his antlers had finished growing but before he left the area to migrate to his winter range.